To Mom.
Thanks for all the chores!

INTRODUCTION   5
USING THIS BOOK   9
DO NOT PANIC!   13

PART ONE: 14

WHAT TO CLEAN AND HOW   14

DAILY CHORES   16
WEEKLY CLEANING   24
MONTHLY CLEANING   39
EVERY THREE MONTHS   56
ANNUALLY   68

PART TWO: 75

FINDING YOUR ROUTINE   75

EXAMPLES OF CLEANING ROUTINES   76
THE TRADITIONAL ROUTINE   77
THE "LITTLE EACH DAY" ROUTINE   81
THE WEEKENDER ROUTINE   84
THE PERFECTIONIST   86
CREATING YOUR PERSONALIZED ROUTINE   89
STRUCTURING YOUR ROUTINE TO FIT YOUR SCHEDULE   95
YOUR PERSONALIZED WEEKLY ROUTINE   97

PART THREE: 99

CHECKLISTS AND RECIPES   99

CLEANING CHECKLISTS   100
CLEANING RECIPES   123

HAPPY CLEANING!   137

ABOUT THE AUTHOR   137
OTHER BOOKS BY KATIE BERRY   138

Cleaning On *Your* Schedule

by Katie Berry

Introduction

Life is hectic. Whether you work outside the home or in it, it often feels like a nonstop race from one crisis to the next. When the day ends, we all long for peace and a break from the madness. You want your home to provide that sanctuary, the calm and comforting space where we can regroup and recover from life's daily demands.

But what if home is anything *but* a haven? What if the dirty dishes and countertop smears, dust and the carpet stains all feel like an accusation that we aren't doing enough? That we're not entitled to rest and relax because there's all this *mess* we should deal with?

Finding time to clean can feel overwhelming.

When you've had a long, stressful workday that's part of an even longer and more stressful week, the last thing you want to do is clean.

Maybe that's why so many of us put it off for the weekend. Then we spend two hectic days cramming in chores, laundry, and errands. Come Monday, we wonder why we still feel so stressed. It's because we never had the chance to relax!

Maybe you've figured out that weekends are better spent doing fun things, only to spend your weekdays scrubbing and dusting yet never feeling like anything is quite ever clean.

Let me tell you two secrets: it's not your fault, and you are not alone.

Not everyone learned how to clean house efficiently.

For years, I've been writing Housewife How-Tos, a blog where I help busy people turn their homes into havens. I teach people how to clean properly and yet efficiently, so they can get their homes under control without giving up the rest of their life. In short, I teach people how to do home better.

It probably sounds like a crazy way to make a living. Whenever someone asks what I do there's always an awkward pause after my answer. It doesn't last for long, though.

In the next breath, they usually say: *"I wish my house was clean"* or *"I have such a hard time fitting cleaning in."*

Believe me, I understand: we all feel that way, even me!

Sometimes they ask questions, like: *"Can you tell me how to keep my house from becoming a mess as soon as I'm done cleaning?"* or *"Do you know how to get (a stain) out of (some item)?"* or, quite often, *"Will you come clean my house for me?"*

The answers, incidentally, are yes, yes, and no but I'll show you how to do it without driving yourself mad.

Don't get me wrong: I don't think that knowing a speedy way to deal with shower mildew or get rid of pee stains on mattresses makes me better than anyone. Those are just skills I've picked up in decades of keeping house and raising my kids -- one of whom really had a problem with mattresses!

Some people are great at knitting. Some folks know how to fix cars. Others can solve complex mathematical equations. I am *awful* at all those things – especially math.

I wrote this book for those who find cleaning a chore.

Thanks to being raised by a single, working mom who was also a perfectionist neat-freak, I know how to clean. And thanks to being more interested in voraciously reading epic fantasy novels and sighing over Shaun Cassidy's latest picture in *Teen Beat*, I learned to clean quickly while still meeting a neat-freak's standards.

Since I wasn't allowed to do either of those things unless the house was clean, I came up with a schedule that let me clean to my mother's standards while still having time to read and day-dream about being Mrs. Shaun Cassidy.

That was all 30-plus years ago. (Yikes!)

That same schedule got me through my first years of marriage and raising my own children. Honestly, until I was struggling to keep a nice house for my family while also having time for my own interests, I'd been a bit resentful of how many chores I'd had as a kid.

So, although my mother encouraged me to learn typing so I'd always have a skill to fall back on, neither of us could have imagined the chores she'd given me would become my most important skills.

Thanks, Mom!

Using This Book

I've structured this book in three parts that form a natural progression that guides you through understanding what all needs to be cleaned – and how to clean it – to creating your own personalized routine that lets you clean on *your* schedule.

First, we'll talk about how to clean various things in your home and how often the need cleaning. Then we'll explore different routines, including the pros and cons of each, to find one that works with *your* schedule. Once you know how to clean and have designed your personalized routine you can use the checklists to get it done quickly so you've got time to do what you enjoy.

The difference between obsessing, cleaning, and tidying

There's a very good reason I spend Part One helping you understand *how* to clean. I could say "dust the living room", for instance, and some people would go dust every little thing, from the ceiling fan to the backsides of bookcases. Others would run a cloth over the tabletops and call it done.

Some people think the first example is how a room should be cleaned every time, and maybe they do it that way for a week or two. Before long, they realize that method of "cleaning" takes a long time, so they put it off. And off. Then the house begins to resemble a disaster zone so they jump back into spending entire days cleaning, wear themselves out, and the cycle continues.

That's not cleaning. It's obsessing.

As for the second example, well, if you've ever asked a child under the age of 17 to clean their room you've probably seen them do something similar. They'll spend an hour in there and tell you it's clean, then you discover they vacuumed around piles of dirty clothes on their floor and shoved the rest under the bed.

That's not cleaning. It's tidying. (Barely.)

The kind of regular cleaning routine that will get your home under control lies somewhere between the two. Yes, we'll get to the point where you're cleaning

those ceiling fans and the backsides of bookcases –
but not on a weekly basis!

**This book is about finding a workable, sustainable
routine that fits *your* life** -- and by "fitting your life"
I mean a schedule that doesn't keep you busy
cleaning every waking minute. After reading this
book you'll know how to have a clean home *and*
have time to enjoy it, too!

This is not a book about organizing.

Before we jump into the good stuff, I want to be
perfectly clear: this book isn't about organizing your
home. Cleaning and organizing are two very
different, though not entirely unrelated, things.

Cleaning is about removing dirt, dust, stains, spills,
and the like. Organizing is about arranging what's left
so that it's easily accessible and maybe even
attractive.

A clean home is not necessarily organized, and an
organized home is not necessarily clean.

In a clean home, the kitchen and bathrooms may be
disinfected and sparkling, the beds made with fresh
sheets, the furniture and floors free of dust and pet

hair, but you *still* can't find a working ballpoint pen or the kids' overdue library books.

On the other hand, an organized home can have dry goods stored in pretty canisters arranged alphabetically in the pantry, t-shirts folded like neat envelopes and vertically filed in dresser drawers, and books arranged by color on the shelves, but your feet stick to the floor as you walk and odors from the garbage disposal fill the air.

In fact, one of the reasons that cleaning overwhelms many people is because they get distracted by trying to organize -- and vice versa!

This book is about finding a routine that works, not a fast solution.

If you're using the "Look inside!" option on Amazon before buying the paperback, or have downloaded a sample of the Kindle book, I want to let you know now that this isn't a quick-fix book.

This book will show you what to clean on a daily, weekly, monthly, quarterly, and annual basis. It will help you fit those tasks into your busy life using checklists that make cleaning thorough and efficient.

If you'd rather get your *entire* house under control in a prompt fashion, then I'd encourage you to use my book <u>30 Days to a Clean and Organized House</u> instead.

Once you've got everything clean and organized, come back to this one to create a personalized routine that will keep your home continually clean. I think you'll find they work brilliantly together!

DO NOT PANIC!

As you read through Part One's descriptions of all the things in your home that need to be cleaned, **do not panic**. Yes, this section contains a lot of information – it also contains a lot of tips to speed things up while *still* thoroughly cleaning your home.

No one is saying you must do *every* step – only you can decide how detailed you want to be. That's something we'll cover in Part 2 when you create your personalized cleaning routine. So **do not panic.**

Think of Part One as a reference section: it's there to clarify what the cleaning checklists in Part Three mean and to provide tips to make cleaning faster.

PART ONE:

WHAT TO CLEAN AND HOW

I don't think I'm going out on a limb here by guessing that you want a home that looks and feels clean but you don't want to spend hours every day on it.

You'd probably also enjoy feeling confident, not ashamed, if someone drops by for a visit.

Maybe you even wish you could throw a party or invite house guests for without wearing yourself out getting your home ready for company.

You can have all of that, and it doesn't have to take up every minute of your time! You just need to find a routine that allows you to clean on *your* schedule.

In this section, we're going to look individually at all the chores involved in cleaning a home. **I strongly encourage you to read through this section before jumping to the Cleaning Checklists.**

This section explains the steps in the checklists. It also gives you an understanding of what's involved so you can be realistic when creating your personalized routine.

Most importantly, this section makes it clear why *consistency* in your cleaning routine is important. With consistency, cleaning goes from taking hours to minutes. With consistency, you have time to add monthly, quarterly, and annual chores into your routine. With consistency, you never, ever have to set aside a week for Spring or Fall Cleaning again.

I know it's tempting to plunge straight into the *doing* part, which is what the Cleaning Checklists cover, but you'll be missing some valuable, time-saving tips and tricks if you do.

Ready to get started? Let's do this!

DAILY CHORES

If you've been struggling to find a routine that lets you clean on your schedule, chances are you've been going through the obsessive/burnout cycle discussed previously. Break that cycle by understanding the *bare minimum* you need to do daily. Add in the "nice touches" when and if you have time and you'll soon find your home meeting your standards with much less time and effort.

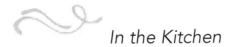 *In the Kitchen*

Dishes: Your home will *never* look clean if dirty dishes crowd your sink and counters.

If you've got a dishwasher, make a habit of emptying it first thing in the morning, maybe while the coffee brews or the kids eat their breakfast. Then, as you use dishes throughout the day, rinse and immediately put them into the dishwasher to keep your sink empty.

If you don't have a dishwasher, consider adopting the British practice of keeping a washing-up bowl filled with soapy water in your sink. As you dirty a utensil or dish, wash and put them away immediately. Replace the water when it gets mucky. Your sink will never be full of dirty dishes, but keeping them clean won't leave your sink a mess, either.

Sink: Kitchen sinks are nasty. In most homes, there's more e. Coli in the kitchen sink than in the toilet after it's flushed. That's due, in part, to food splatters but also because many people use the kitchen sink to wash their hands.

So, they need to be cleaned at *least* once a day. It doesn't need to be a difficult process. Squirt some soap onto a dishcloth and give every surface in the sink a good rub, including in the drain recess. Rinse with hot water and you've removed most bacteria already.

>> **TIP** *Use the Daily Sink Spray (in the recipe section) between scrubbings and you'll prevent kitchen odors and keep fruit flies from breeding in your drain, too.*

Counters: Keeping counters tidy makes your kitchen look cleaner than it is. They're easier to clean, too, and you'll deter kitchen pests like cockroaches and ants.

Wipe your counters daily using a microfiber cloth and an all-purpose spray. (See the recipe section.) This does *not* mean you've got to move everything on your counter -- just make a point to clean as much of it as you can.

» TIP *Reducing the number of small appliances on your counters to just those you use daily will free up a lot of counter space. If you don't have room in your cupboards for all your gadgets, it's time to ask some hard questions about the ones you're holding onto.*

Do you use them regularly or just for special occasions? If the latter, is there something else you could use instead? Just because you paid "good money" to buy a gadget, or were given it, doesn't mean you should keep it.

Why pay good money via a mortgage or rent to house something that's not useful? Give it to a friend, sell it online, or donate it to charity and you'll feel better about letting it go.

Kitchen floor: In an ideal world, we'd all sweep and mop our kitchen floors nightly. I don't have the time or energy for that, and I bet you don't, either.

If you live in a dusty area or have pets, go over your floor with a dust-catching cloth or sweeper of some kind once a day. Then use a microfiber cloth and all-purpose spray on any spills.

And, hey, if you've got the time and energy to do a full sweep and mop every night give yourself a pat on the back… then come do mine.

>> **TIP** *You can find out about the one I use, and other cleaning tools I love, on the "Recommended Products" page of HousewifeHowTos.com.*

Sponges, dishcloths, and towels: To prevent cross-contamination, these things must be cleaned daily.

For sponges, get them soaking wet and stick them in the microwave on HIGH for 2 minutes or soak them in a 50-50 solution of hot water and vinegar.

Dishcloths and kitchen towels should be changed daily, and more often after greasy meals. If you hand-dry dishes, make a point to keep separate towels for hand-drying.

>> **TIP** *If your kitchen dishcloths tend to get smelly be sure that after each use you're washing them in hot, soapy water and wringing them well. Then*

spread them out, perhaps on the sink divider, so they dry thoroughly.

There are certainly additional things you can add to your daily once-over in the kitchen like wiping down small appliances and cleaning appliance fronts if you want. Are they necessary? Not if you're consistently cleaning your kitchen each week.

 *In the Bedroom*

Make the beds. As the largest piece of furniture in the room, the bed is a focal point. No matter how clean your room is, it will look messy if the bed isn't made. On the other hand, making your bed will give the impression your room is clean even if it's not. **Put dirty clothes into the hamper.** A floor strewn with laundry will also make your room look dirty. If you aren't in the habit of putting clothes directly into the hamper after removing them, at least scoop them up in the morning.

Take water glasses and dishes to the kitchen. Many of us like to keep a glass of water on our nightstands to sip if we wake during the night with a dry mouth or a cough. Some of us like to snack in bed, too (don't judge me), but those dishes shouldn't remain in your room or they'll attract pests.

Optional additional daily cleaning tasks in the bedroom include running a carpet sweeper or vacuum over high-traffic areas and misting the sheets with linen spray (see Recipes) so they smell fresh every night.

 *In the Bathroom*

Deal with toilet messes. Without getting into graphic detail, this means scrubbing away any streaks in the bowl or splatters on the seat or floor – something you're probably quite familiar with if you've ever potty-trained a boy.

>> **TIP** *Keep a container of disinfecting wipes in the bathroom and a toilet brush near the commode so you can quickly deal with messes when you find them.*

Sinks: We all know the purpose of washing our hands after using the bathroom, but think about what we're washing off them. In short: there's a lot of disgusting bacteria in there! Use the Daily Sink Spray in the recipes section to keep them disinfected and odor-free.

Hand towels: Unfortunately, not everyone is good about hands properly. (I hear that singing the alphabet song while washing hands does the trick.) This means that hand towels collect a lot of yucky stuff, too -- so change them daily.

Optional finishing touches include buffing water spots from the mirror and fixtures with a microfiber cloth, using a Daily Shower Spray (see Recipes) to prevent mildew, and wiping the vanity with a dry cloth to pick up hairs and makeup powders.

Living/Family Room or Lounge

Dishes to the sink. Again, this is about pest control as much as it's about clutter.

Wipe up spills and crumbs. A damp microfiber cloth makes this easy and will keep your tabletops looking nice.

Pick up trash. I used to be the only one in my family who ever thought to do this, while everyone else complained it was a hassle to walk food wrappers or other trash to the kitchen garbage. I put an attractive wastebasket next to the sofa. Now it's easier for me to do but apparently not for them. Sound familiar?

To keep your living/family room continually ready for drop-by visitors, you could also straighten DVDs, CDs, etc., fold throw blankets and straighten pillows, and run a carpet sweeper or vacuum over high-traffic areas. But don't add those tasks if your daily routine is already full.

Laundry

If you have a washer/dryer, do a load of laundry every day. This practice will go a *long* way to freeing up your weekends and ending the "Where's my favorite shirt?" emergencies.

Plus, if you're changing your kitchen cloths and bathroom hand towels daily, and your bed linens weekly, it's the only way to keep up.

As for those who don't own their own washer/dryer, don't fret. You no doubt already have enough linens and clothes to get you through the week.

WEEKLY CLEANING

The key to weekly tasks is consistency. I can't emphasize that enough: **cleaning on a regular schedule, even when the room looks nice, makes cleaning go faster**.

That said, depending on the number of people and pets in your home, and how well they do picking up after themselves, you might not need to clean all these rooms weekly.

In homes without small children, for instance, you can often go two weeks or more before needing to clean the living/family room or lounge. The same goes for bedrooms, though you should still change your bed linens weekly.

Again, at this stage we're covering what needs to be cleaned and how to clean it. In Part 2 you'll discover, based on *your* home, which rooms need to be cleaned every week and which you can comfortably clean less often.

Pick up clutter and trash. Kitchen counters and tables tend to be dumping grounds for everything people carry into the home. Unfortunately, these piles make cleaning the kitchen a hassle. Rather than spending time dealing with them before you clean, scoop them into a bag or basket for now. If something is obviously trash, dispose of it immediately.

Clean the sink. If you've been good about scrubbing your sink and keeping it empty throughout the week this will only take a minute. Sprinkle on a scouring powder – even baking soda (bicarbonate of soda for UK readers) – will work. Use a microfiber cloth and rub in circles to dislodge grime and buff away utensil marks. Rinse, then use the Daily Sink Spray on the sink and faucets to disinfect them. Wait 1 minute and buff dry.

Garbage disposal. If not cleaned regularly, your garbage disposal will smell awful and work poorly. To clean it, prime your faucet by running the water until the stream is hot. Turn the water off and drop a handful of ice cubes or egg shells in the disposal, sprinkle in some coarse salt, and run the disposal with the cold water going full blast. This scours away any food buildup and grease. Switch to hot water to flush.

Next, turn the disposal off and wait for the blades to stop spinning. Using your fingers, gently pry open the rubber flanges so you can see their undersides. Use hot, soapy water and a small scrub brush to dislodge any grime or biofilm then rinse with hot water and return the flanges to place.

>> **TIP** *Running a few thin slices of lemon in your disposal every few days will keep it smelling fresh, too.*

Spray and wipe surfaces. One of the basic rules of cleaning efficiently is working the room from left to right, top to bottom, so you only make one pass. Remember this as you spray and wipe surfaces in your kitchen. I like to start at the door but you can certainly pick your own starting point.

While it's impossible for me to know everything you might have in your kitchen that needs cleaning (and it would be creepy if I did), here are some things that should be sprayed and wiped *every* week:

- Cupboard doors and handles
- Drawer fronts and handles
- Countertops
- Backsplash
- Small appliances
- Canisters and other items on the counter
- Range hood and stove top
- Oven door and handle
- Spills on the oven floor
- Appliance fronts
- Top of refrigerator
- Light switches
- Door knobs
- Phone
- Outside of garbage can

Clean the microwave: You don't need a cutesy gadget to clean your microwave! Just fill a large mug or measuring cup with water and a splash of white vinegar or a few slices of lemon. Put this in the center of the microwave and heat it on HIGH for 2 minutes. Wait another minute for the steam work.

Open the microwave, carefully dump the mug of water, and use a microfiber cloth to wipe away the loosened grime. If you have a turntable, remove and wash it in hot, soapy water.

>> **TIP** *Reduce food splatters in the microwave by using paper towels or flexible screens to cover food when cooking. See the Recommended Products page on HousewifeHowTos.com for the ones I use, as well as other cleaning tools that I love.*

Refrigerator and freezer: Toss out any spoiled food. If you're in doubt, the rule of thumb is that greasy foods go bad after 2 days, others after 4.

Wipe spills and drips using a microfiber cloth dipped in hot, soapy water.

Replace the paper towels lining your crisper drawer.

Wash the drawer used to hold raw meat (which should be the bottom drawer so there's no risk of bacteria-laden drips contaminating the rest of your food).

Take out the trash. Even pricey kitchen bin liners sometimes split, so it's a good idea to line the bottom of your bin with old newspaper to catch any spills. Change this weekly and give the outside of the can a thorough cleaning. The homemade Disinfectant Spray and a microfiber cloth do a great job on this!

*» **TIP** Kitchen trash cans need to be washed, though not necessarily on a weekly basis. If you can wash them outside, all the better.*

Where I live, it gets cold enough in the winter that we must shut the outside water off, so I wash my kitchen trash can with hot, soapy in the bathtub before cleaning the bathroom. Once it's dry, I spray it well with homemade and let it air dry before returning it to the kitchen.

Clean the floor. Pick up everything on the floor. Turn the chairs or stools upside down on the table to get them out of the way. Sweep or vacuum the floor, paying extra attention to the edges of the room and food preparation areas.

Mop the floor. If you use a disposable mopping pad be sure to check it every 10 feet or so and switch to a clean one as needed. If you use a standard mop, or like to scrub floors on hands and knees, there's a great Homemade Floor Cleaner in the recipe section. I use a steam mop because it's easier on my back and fast!

Deal with that clutter. Remember the clutter you scooped up before cleaning the kitchen? Now, while the floor dries, is the time to deal with it. Separate it into piles based on the room it belongs in and return everything to its place.

>> **TIP** *If your kids drive you crazy because they leave stuff on the kitchen counter, consider having them do a few chores to earn their stuff back. You'll get a little help around the house, and they'll learn that leaving stuff lying around leads to extra work for them, too! You can find a printable* list of Chores that Kids *on HousewifeHowTos.com to can hang on your fridge.*

Finish up. Put a new liner in the trash can. Set out fresh kitchen towels.

 *Bathroom Weekly Cleaning*

Bathrooms need to be cleaned and disinfected once a week. If someone in the family has a flu or stomach virus, you'll want to treat the toilet, sink, vanity and tub daily until they're well.

Declutter the counters. Return toiletries and brushes to their proper spot. Set anything that doesn't belong in the bathroom outside the door. Put all trash into the can. Remove everything else from the vanity and tub surround so they're completely clear.

Pretreat. You'll find cleaning bathroom surfaces goes *much* faster if you go over them with a dry microfiber cloth first to pick up hair, powders, and lint. Doing so means that once you start using a spray you'll get the surfaces clean, rather than moving hair from one spot to another. Be sure to dust the light fixture while you're at it.

>> **TIP** *Always use a different cloth to clean the toilet, even when you're simply wiping it down as part of pretreatment. I use microfiber cloths that come in three different colors and reserve the yellow ones for the toilet so I don't have to worry about spreading nastiness from one place to the next.*

Spray surfaces. Spray disinfecting cleaner into the toilet bowl then spray the vanity, sinks, faucets, tub and tub surround, shower walls, and shower door. Go back and scrub then flush the toilet bowl while the spray does its thing, then spray the toilet tank, outside of the bowl, seat, and both sides of the lid.

Wipe. Use a clean, damp cloth to wipe the vanity and faucets. Rinse the cloth and wipe the sinks. Switch cloths to clean the tub and tub surround or the shower walls and shower floor (or both, depending on your home). Switch cloths again and wipe all surfaces of the toilet, tank, lid, and seat.

Make it sparkle. Using a microfiber cloth and glass cleaner, clean the mirror from top to bottom. Use the same cloth to buff faucets and other chrome or shiny surfaces.

Clean the floor. Pick up and shake any bathroom rugs to dislodge hair. Set them outside the door to launder. Sweep or vacuum the floor then mop using your preferred method.

Finish up. Wash the bathroom rugs as a separate load of laundry. (If you don't have small children you can put this off to every couple of weeks.) Sort the pile of things that belong elsewhere, group it by room, and return it to where it belongs.

Empty the trash can and spray it with disinfecting spray. Once it's dry, add a paper towel or liner and return it to the bathroom.

Set out fresh towels and launder the dirty ones.

Check the supply of toilet paper and toiletries, adding more as needed to get through the week.

» TIP *If mildew is a problem in your shower, use the Daily Shower Spray recipe during your daily routine. Also, make a habit of running the bathroom fan for 10 minutes after each use to reduce humidity.*

 *Living / Family Room Weekly Cleaning*

Straighten up. Pick up the trash, including old magazines and newspapers, and set it outside the door. Do the same with things that belong in another room. Return CDs, DVDs, books, etc. to their proper spot. Fold blankets.

Dust. Open the curtains and give them a good shake to dislodge dust and pet hair. Close the blinds and dust them, then open them in the other direction (if you have bi-louver blinds) and dust that side, too.

Now, work your way around the room left to right, top to bottom, dusting then polishing. (See the Recipes section for homemade furniture polish.) Be sure to get:

- TV screen
- Window casings and sills
- Door jambs and doors

- Furniture
- Knickknacks
- Lamps, lamp shades, and bulbs

Clean smudges. Use a clean, damp microfiber cloth to wipe light switches, door knobs, door jambs, and smudges on the walls. Use a disinfecting wipe on the TV remote.

Vacuum. Use the dust or upholstery attachment to vacuum the sofa, chairs, lamp shades, and throw pillows. Use the crevice attachment to get around the base of walls and heavy furniture where a lot of dust and pet hair collect. Vacuum the rest of the floor and any throw rugs.

Finish up. Discard trash, putting recyclables in their appropriate bin. Sort the pile of things that belong elsewhere by room and return them to place.

Bedroom Weekly Cleaning

Pick up clutter and trash. If you've been good about doing daily chores this won't take long! Put trash in the can and gather items that belong elsewhere. Set both outside the door. Return dishes and water glasses to the kitchen.

Dust. Remove your bedspread or duvet but leave the sheets in place to protect your mattress while you dust. Give the curtains a good shake to dislodge dust and pet hair, and open them. Now, working left to right and top to bottom, be sure to dust:

- Blinds (both sides)
- Window casings and sills
- Furniture
- Knickknacks
- Mirror
- Wall art
- Lamps, lamp shades, and bulbs

Clean smudges. Use a clean, damp microfiber cloth to wipe light switches, door knobs, door jambs, and smudges on the walls. Use a disinfecting wipe on the TV remote.

Change the sheets. Strip the bed and set the dirty linens outside the bedroom door. Make your bed with fresh sheets.

» **TIP** *If putting on pillow cases is a struggle, try the trick that hotel maids use -- lay the pillow on the bed* *and give it a karate chop vertically down the center. Gather the corners with one hand and slip the pillow case over them with the other. Now you can slide the case over the rest of the pillow easily.*

Vacuum. Use the dust/upholstery attachment to vacuum lamp shades plus pet beds or armchairs if you have them in your bedroom. Use the crevice attachment around the base of the walls. Vacuum the rest of the floor, including under the bed if you can.

Finish up. Launder the dirty sheets. Empty the trash and return the wastebasket to your bedroom. Group items that belong elsewhere by room and return them to where they belong.

>> **TIP** *Laundering a room's linens on the same day you clean the room – whether that's kitchen or bathroom towels or bedsheets – goes a long way to reducing how much laundry you must do over the weekend. It also ensures you've got clean spares should you get ill. It happens!*

Deal with clutter. Pick up any trash and put it in a bag. Collect items that belong elsewhere and set them aside.

Wipe and polish. Entrance doors develop a lot of smudges. Spray and wipe these with a microfiber cloth. Be sure to clean the doorknobs inside and out, too. Dust and clean any other furniture in the entry, such as a Parson's bench or coat rack.

» **TIP** *If you're constantly dealing with a pile of shoes by the door consider using an attractive boot tray or low, horizontal shoe rack there to contain them.*

Shake and sweep. Shake the mats outdoors and give them a quick sweep with the broom or a once-over with the vacuum.

Clean the floor. Sweep or vacuum the floor paying particular attention around the edges. Mop and let the floor completely dry before returning mats to place.

>> **TIP** *Did you know most household dust enters our homes on the bottoms of peoples' shoes? Keeping a mat on both the inside and outside of every entrance goes a long way to reducing dust in the house. Banning shoes indoors helps, too!*

MONTHLY CLEANING

By now you're realizing that daily and weekly cleaning cover most of your home, but there are still some things we haven't touched yet. These monthly tasks can certainly be done more often, but they don't need to be.

Can you put them off even longer than that? Sure, but then you're back to piling up tasks and will wind up having to set aside a week for Spring or Fall Cleaning.

Once you've established a habit of doing daily chores and a regular, weekly cleaning schedule you'll find that cleaning the bathroom, for instance, begins to take less time – 10 minutes, for instance, instead of a half-hour or more.

That means you can squeeze in a monthly task or two in the *same* amount of time you'd previously spent. Maybe even less!

Trash cans. I've mentioned previously that we should wash trash cans anytime the liner leaks and leaves a nasty pool of sludge. Even if that doesn't happen, it's a good idea to wash your garbage can.

This is a great project to schedule immediately before you clean the bathroom: just wash the can in hot, soapy water in the tub and rinse. Spray it with disinfecting spray and let it air dry. Once you're done, give the tub a thorough cleaning, too.

Refrigerator and freezer. This task isn't just about dealing with spills like we do in the weekly chores. A monthly cleaning involves removing all food from the fridge and freezer and washing the shelves. Be sure to stash that food in coolers while you work so it remains at a food safe temperature!

Once the shelves are clean, unplug the unit and pull it out from the wall. (Get help if you need it.) Vacuum the coils, dust the wall behind the unit, and wipe up any messes on the floor. Plug it back in and return the unit to place.

Wait an hour for it to reach proper temperature, add a fresh paper towel to the bottom of your crisper and meat drawers, then put your food back inside.

This attention will keep your refrigerator/freezer in top working condition while lowering energy bills, too. As a bonus, you'll also know exactly what's in your freezer so you can use it.

>> **TIP** *To deodorize and clean your refrigerator/ freezer at the same time, wash the shelves and drawers with hot, soapy water to which you've added a sprinkle of baking soda (bicarbonate of soda).*

Drains. Even if you're good about pouring bacon fat and other grease into a tin can and tossing it into the trash, kitchen drains still collect a lot of grease. Over time, that can reduce drainage. It also attracts fruit flies and other pests. That's why it's a good idea to clean your drains once a month.

Prime the tap by running the faucet until hot water comes out. Turn the water off.

Sprinkle one-half cup of baking soda (bicarbonate of soda) into each drain and then add 2 cups of hot vinegar *slowly*. Beware: this is going to foam in your sink just like it did in that volcano you made for your

5th grade science class! That foaming action will lift away grime.

Once the bubbling stops, run the hot water for 2 minutes and turn on the disposal, if you have one.

Dishwasher. It's odd to think that a machine which swirls detergent and hot water around can get dirty, but it's true. Not just dirty, either: if left untended, food debris can build up and clog the jets so your dishes don't get truly clean. To keep that from happening, give the dishwasher a good cleaning once a month.

Remove the racks and look in the bottom of the machine for any food chunks, bones, or other debris. Be careful: I've found broken glass in the bottom of mine!

Take out the food catcher – it looks like a round piece that sticks up from the bottom of the machine. Most need to be turned counter-clockwise before they're pulled out. Wash this in hot, soapy water and return it to place.

Give the sprayer jets a spin with your hand to make sure they're moving freely.

You should also look in the jet holes to make sure nothing is lodged in them. (I once found a broken off toothpick, presumably from a martini. That'll teach me to load the dishes after having friends over for cocktails!) Use pliers or tweezers to pull out anything you find.

Using your fingers, gently spread the door gasket and wipe it with a damp microfiber cloth using hot, soapy water. If you find a lot of mineral buildup, you may need to scrub it with a small brush and a 50-50 solution of vinegar and water then go over it again with the damp cloth.

Shut the door and press the "Drain/Cancel" button to fully empty the machine. After 2 minutes, open the door and pour 2 cups of white distilled vinegar directly into the bottom of the machine.

Close the door and run the shortest cycle your machine offers. The vinegar will clean away soap residue, neutralize odors, and kill any mold and mildew spores.

Once the machine has finished running, return the racks to position. Now it's good to go!

>> **TIP** *If your machine has a reservoir for a rinsing agent, you can fill this with straight white distilled vinegar. It does the same job but also prevents bacterial growth and odors -- and it costs a lot less!*

Oven. Listen, nobody likes cleaning the oven. Nobody. Okay, well, maybe there's some crazy person who finds it somehow rewarding but I've never met that person and, to be honest, would probably fear them. Still, the oven must be cleaned because, you know, fires are bad and stuff.

Remove the racks.

If you have a self-cleaning oven use that setting – though it's going to fill your home with some noxious odors which some people say are harmful. It's your call.

If you're cleaning the oven manually, use a rubber spatula to dislodge burnt-on food. Wipe this away with a damp paper towel. (You can use your vacuum's dust brush if you'd rather, but you'll want to wash the brush well afterward.)

Use a paste of baking soda (bicarbonate of soda) and hot water to scour any remaining spills then wipe the area with a clean, damp paper towel. Repeat for stains on the inside of the door, too.

Very stubborn spots might require a soak before they come up. Do this by placing a paper towel dampened with a 50-50 mixture of hot water over the spot for a half-hour. You should be able to wipe away the mess now.

» **TIP** *Ordinarily, I don't recommend paper towels for cleaning. They're wasteful, and the use of them is an added household expense. Paper towels also leave behind bits of lint and even the best of them doesn't have the scrubbing power of a microfiber cloth.*

When it comes to cleaning the oven, though, I go for paper towels rather than running the risk of greasy, permanent stains on my microfiber cloths.

Laundry room and machines

Whether your laundry room is vast and beautifully appointed or in kitchen, which is prevalent in the UK, the laundry area tends to get covered in fine lint.

Meanwhile, the washer is prone to developing odors while the dryer, if not cleaned regularly, poses a fire hazard. Just more reasons to hate doing the laundry, right?

Once a month, wipe the exterior of both machines with a dry microfiber cloth to pick up lint. Use another dry cloth to go over any shelves, wall décor, windows, blinds, and door jamb.

Use a clean, damp microfiber cloth to wipe the shelves and any smudges on the window sills, door and doorjamb, blinds, and walls. Wipe the machines down, too.

Open the washing machine then clean the inside of the lid with a microfiber cloth and all-purpose spray. If your detergent dispenser is removable, take it out and wash it in the sink using hot water and a small scrub brush.

For top-loading machines, spray a microfiber cloth with all-purpose spray and run it around the top of the drum inside the unit. You'll be surprised what collects there!

For front-loading machines, gently pry the door gasket open with your fingers and use a microfiber with all-purpose spray to clean soap residue and buildup.

Clean the inside of the drum with a microfiber cloth dipped in a 50-50 mixture of water and white distilled vinegar. Get it good and wet so the vinegar has a chance to kill mold and mildew spores. Leave the lid or door open and let the drum air dry.

Open the dryer and remove the lint filter. Wash this in hot, soapy water in the kitchen or utility sink and let it air dry. Meanwhile, wipe the inside of the dryer drum and door with a microfiber cloth and a 50-50 water and vinegar mix. Pay special attention to the sensor unit so you don't damage it. Let the dryer drum air dry.

Use a flexible lint brush or a dryer vent attachment for your vacuum cleaner to get down into the dryer and remove lint. (Be gentle about it or you'll just spread the stuff everywhere.)

Return the lint filter to place.

Unplug the machines and pull them out from the wall. Clean the floor and wall behind the machine. Unhook the dryer vent hose and clean any lint you find. Replace the hose, plug the machines in, and return them to position.

Sweep and mop.

Garage

This is where I want to remind you that cleaning is not the same thing as organizing. If your garage is a chaotic dumping ground it *will* be difficult, but not impossible, to clean.

If you need help organizing your garage, there is a detailed printable which covers both cleaning and organizing on my blog. Search for "Garage Spring Cleaning Checklist" on HousewifeHowTos.com.

As far as monthly cleaning, you'll want to pull your car(s) out then sweep the ceiling and walls since garages are often full of cobwebs.

Dust the light fixtures, clean smudges on the walls, door, and door jamb, and pick up any trash.

Next, treat oil spills on the floor by sprinkling them with clay-based kitty litter or baking soda. Let this sit for an hour (overnight is even better) and sweep it up. Remove any remaining oil by scrubbing with hot, soapy water. Be *very* careful since wet cement floors are extremely slippery!

Once the treated areas have dried, shake out your entrance mats and sweep the rest of the floor before pulling your car(s) back in.

Car

Though technically not part of the house, many of us spend so much time in our cars that it feels like we live in them. A little monthly attention can make a miserable commute just a bit more bearable, so don't neglect to take care of your ride.

First, get the junk out. Throw away any trash, and gather things that don't belong in your car. Put these aside for now. Remove the floor mats and set them aside, too.

Using your vacuum's upholstery or dust brush attachment, vacuum the ceiling, seats, beneath the seats, the console, dash, cup holders, and floor. (Yes, the ceiling: a lot of odors gather there!)

Switch to the vacuum's crevice attachment and clean between the seats and console. Use your hand to fish around in the fold at the base of seats to make sure there are no coins or small toys in there, then wedge the crevice attachment in the fold to vacuum it as well.

Use a damp microfiber cloth to wipe down the dash, console, door panels, seat belt buckles, steering wheel, gear shift, and other hard surfaces (but not the windows).

To treat carpet and upholstery stains, combine 1 cup warm water, 1 cup white distilled vinegar, and 1 teaspoon liquid dish soap in a spray bottle. (I recommend using Dawn if you're in the US or Fairy in the UK as they're brilliant grease-cutters.)

Spray this on stains and gently scrub them with a microfiber cloth or, for tough stains, with a soft scrub brush. Follow with a microfiber cloth dampened with plain water and let dry.

Use a glass cleaner and microfiber cloth on windows and chrome accents.

Give dashboards and leather surfaces a shine with Armor All. If you'd rather make your own, combine equal parts water, white vinegar and baby oil. Shake well and apply with a soft, lint-free cloth then buff again with a separate cloth to bring out the shine.

(Don't worry: these recipes are on the checklist!)

Ceiling fans

It's amazing how much dust these things collect! Of course, you never see it if you keep your ceiling fans running 24/7, but it's there and eventually the buildup will shower down on your furniture. So, clean them.

If your ceiling fans are low enough to reach you can easily clean them by slipping a pillow case over the blades, one at a time, and running it back and forth. The dust will fall into the pillowcase so you can shake it outside then toss the thing in the wash.

On the other hand, if you're short like I am, an extension cleaning kit with a ceiling fan attachment is a great tool to have. All you do is extend the rod, slip the brush over the blade and run it back and forth. Shake the blade outside then rinse it in your sink to keep it clean between uses. Look for a kit that has other attachments to deal with cobwebs and ceilings, too. (See the Recommended Products page on HousewifeHowTos.com for the one I use.)

Blinds

While dusting blinds should be part of your weekly cleaning routine, once a month they need a little extra attention – especially those in the kitchen, which tend to get greasy.

The easiest way to clean them is by wrapping microfiber cloths over the ends of kitchen tongs. Secure them in place with rubber bands.

Fill a bowl with 1 cup warm water, 1 teaspoon liquid dish detergent, and 1 cup rubbing (isopropyl) alcohol (known as surgical spirts in the UK). Dip the cloth-wrapped ends of the tongs in this solution and run them along each slat of the blinds to clean both sides at the same time.

≫TIP *Put a bath towel on the floor under your window to catch drips!*

Baseboards

This is another task where an extension cleaning kit comes in handy – just use the dusting attachment and walk it around your baseboards to remove dust.

No extension cleaning kit? Use the dust brush attachment on your vacuum, or do it the old-fashioned way by grabbing a cloth and crawling around on your hands and knees. (Ouch!)

Unfortunately, to wash baseboards you'll need to do the hands-and-knees thing… or get one of your kids to do it! A damp microfiber cloth should be sufficient for most homes. Add a squirt of liquid dish detergent to clean stubborn stains.

Vacuum cleaner

Yes, your vacuum cleaner needs to be cleaned. It sounds finicky, but think of all the messes we use this machine to pick up: dust, lint, pet and human hair, clothing threads, carpet fibers, food crumbs, etc. These can build up and reduce the machine's suction. Keep yours in good shape with a quick monthly cleaning.

Unplug the machine. Spread newspapers or an old sheet on the floor where you'll be working since this process will produce quite a bit of dirt.

Remove the plate over the roller brush. Pull or snip away any threads or hairs that are wrapped around the brush then wash it in a sink of hot, soapy water. Rinse and let the brush air dry.

Use a stiff-bristled brush to dislodge any caked-on dirt in the air passages and brush housing. Use a microfiber cloth and hot, soapy water to wipe away remaining residue. Replace the brush roller once it's dry and reattach the plate.

Remove any filters. Most modern vacuums have filters that can be washed in warm, soapy water. Check your manual to see if yours can be washed or if they can only be replaced. In general, plastic or foam filters can be washed. Paper filters should be taken outside and shaken well to dislodge dust. Return the filters to place.

Change the bag (if any) when it's 2/3 full to maintain suction. For bagless vacuum cleaners, dump and then wipe the inside of the dustbin with a damp cloth.

Wipe the vacuum exterior, including the wheels, with a damp microfiber cloth. Hand wash the attachments and let them completely dry before putting your machine away.

Most of the tasks which should be done every three months sync nicely with the weekly cleaning routine: they're simply an additional step. By the time you've been cleaning rooms every week for three months you'll find the process is so quick that an additional step doesn't seem like much. So, don't get discouraged by reading this list!

 *Pillows and blankets*

Given how much time we spend in our beds, it's no surprise these things collect a lot of body oils, skin cells, and dust mites. Pillows can also harbor mold and mildew spores, so it's important to wash them regularly.

To clean pillows, place two at a time in the washing machine and launder them with your regular laundry detergent plus one-half cup oxygenated bleach (e.g., Oxiclean) and one-half cup baking soda (bicarbonate of soda).

Run the hottest, longest cycle your machine offers. Add 1 cup vinegar to the rinse. Once the cycle ends, adjust the pillows in the machine and run a second rinse cycle to fully remove any detergent residue.

Transfer the pillows to the dryer and add 2 or 3 clean tennis balls to the load. These will keep the pillow fibers from clumping and fluff your pillows as they dry. Run the dryer for a full cycle, adjust the pillows, then run it for a half-cycle to make sure they're completely dry.

Blankets should be washed individually. Check the manufacturer's label for temperature settings. In general, cotton and synthetic blankets can handle a warm/warm regular cycle but quilts should be washed using the delicate setting and a cold/cold cycle. Use low heat to dry.

 *Mattresses*

Like pillows, our mattresses collect a lot of sweat, body oils, and dead skin cells. These become a veritable buffet for dust mites and can lead to the growth of mold and mildew. Sweet dreams? Not on a dirty mattress, baby. Give yours a good cleaning every 3 months and you'll rest easy.

Strip and vacuum it using the upholstery attachment. Then sprinkle on a thin layer of baking soda (bicarbonate of soda) and, using your hands or a soft-bristled brush, work that into the top fabric. This will pull out moisture and neutralize oils. Wait 10 minutes and vacuum the mattress again.

To remove blood stains, combine 2 oz. of 3% hydrogen peroxide and 1 tablespoon each liquid dish soap and table salt. Gently spread this paste onto the stain and allow it to dry. Scrape away the dried paste with a spoon and vacuum the spot. If any stain remains, dab it with straight hydrogen peroxide and a white cloth until it's gone.

>> **TIP** *Use a white cloth when cleaning stains so you don't transfer dyes from the cloth to the area you're cleaning.*

To remove urine stains, combine 3 tablespoons of baking soda (bicarbonate of soda) with 8 oz. of 3% hydrogen peroxide in a spray bottle. Add a drop of liquid dish soap. Lightly spray the stain – do NOT get it soaking wet! – and wipe repeatedly with a clean, white cloth. Let the area fully dry.

If the urine stain persists after drying, make a paste from 3 tablespoons of powdered laundry detergent and a little water. Spread a very thin layer of this over the stain and let it dry. Scrape the dried paste away with the edge of a spoon then go over the area with a white cloth dipped into hydrogen peroxide. Once the area is dry, vacuum it.

Rotate your mattress end to end every 3 months. Innerspring or coil mattresses should be flipped end to end twice a year, too.

>> TIP *Using a hypoallergenic, waterproof mattress pad will prevent stains and keep your mattress dust-free so you can skip vacuuming.*

Shower curtains and liners

Fabric shower curtains should be laundered per the manufacturer's label. If you can't find the label, use your washing machine's gentle cycle with a cold/cold setting and either skip the dryer or use the no-heat/fluff cycle.

To wash plastic shower curtains or liners, add them to the machine and toss in a few washcloths or hand towels to act as scrubbers on soap scum and grime. Wash using warm water on a regular cycle with one-half cup *each* laundry detergent and baking soda (bicarbonate of soda). To kill mildew spores, pour 1 cup of white distilled vinegar into the machine during the rinse cycle.

 *Medicine cabinet*

Although bathroom medicine cabinets are *horrible* places to store medicines due to the heat and humidity, many of us have no other option. In that case, it's particularly important to discard expired products and replace them with fresh ones to ensure maximum effectiveness. Doing this every 3 months also gives you a chance to purge products you never use or don't like.

 *Coffee machines*

You already wash your coffee machine's pot every day, but it's a good idea to clean the machine's insides to keep it running well. This is easily done by filling the tank with a 50-50 solution of HOT water and HOT white vinegar then brewing a full pot. Discard the vinegar water and run several pots of clear, cool water through the machine to flush away any vinegar smell.

If you have a Keurig, use the same 50-50 solution in the tank, skip the k-Cup, and brew repeated cups until the tank empties. Repeat twice with tanks of plain, cold water. (If your machine is still running slow, or you think it's broken, look for "How To Clean A Keurig" on HousewifeHowTos.com for instructions that have helped *thousands* of people get their machines running like new again.)

 *Windows*

Ugh, right? I hate cleaning them, too. To make it easier, I use a homemade glass cleaner and a squeegee which also attaches to my extension cleaning pole to get tall windows clean without having to climb on a ladder.

Be sure to clean windows on an overcast day, or at least when the sun isn't shining directly on them, or you'll get streaks. It's also a good idea to run the squeegee in different directions on the inside and outside of the window so you can tell which side the streak is on.

» **TIP** *Place a bath towel on the floor beneath windows to keep drips from landing on your carpet.*

 *Shampoo carpets*

I am *always* amazed at how much better my carpets look after they've been shampooed! But there's more to this task than merely filling the tank and running the machine over your carpets. Taking the time to do it properly will get your carpets deep clean and significantly reduce the amount of dust in your home!

Start by vacuuming the room thoroughly. Be sure to use the crevice attachment around the base of the wall.

Pretreat any stains with a solution of 1 cup warm water, 1 cup white vinegar, and one-half teaspoon liquid dish detergent. Dab this onto the stain with a white cloth, wait 5 minutes, then blot with a dry cloth.

Use the carpet shampoo solution recommended by your machine's manufacturer. If you aren't concerned about warranties, use the Homemade Carpet Shampoo in the Recipe section. Be sure to spot test your carpet first! (I've been using that recipe in my machine for years without problems, but I take no responsibility for how it affects your carpets or machine.)

TAKE YOUR TIME when shampooing your carpet – don't just run the machine back and forth. Most machines put solution down as you push the machine forward then suck up dirty water as you pull the machine toward you. It's vital that you pull slowly so you extract the maximum amount of water and dirt.

Run the machine in overlapping sections from one side of your room to the other. Let your carpet dry fully before deciding whether you need to repeat areas. Not waiting will oversaturate your carpet which breaks down the glue holding fibers in place and can cause your padding and subfloor to grow mold.

Once the carpet is fully dry, vacuum it again to fluff the fibers.

 *Air ducts*

A professional air duct cleaning involves shooting hot water through your duct system as a wire brush scours the duct walls. That's great and all, but it's expensive – especially if your ducts are leaky and you wind up having to replace sections of your ceiling.

To clean your own air ducts, remove your floor registers and wash them in hot, soapy water then rinse them well. While they're air drying, slip your vacuum's attachment hose down each vent as far as it can reach and work it around to clean the walls and floor of your air ducts.

For a more thorough cleaning, invest in a rotary brush vent cleaning attachment for your vacuum cleaner. (See the Recommended Products page on HousewifeHowTos.com.) Slip that on your vacuum cleaner's hose and run it down the vent. Do NOT use your vacuum's attachments or you might lose them for good!

Finish by using a damp microfiber cloth to clean as far down the vent as you can reach and then replace the register. Run your whole house fan or HVAC for 10 minutes so the air filter has a chance to catch any dirt you've dislodged, then replace the filter with a clean one.

Bedroom closets

Since this is a book about cleaning, I'm not going to focus on organizing closets beyond encouraging you to purge any clothes that don't fit, don't flatter, don't feel comfortable, or don't make you feel good when you wear them. (I cover closet organization in-depth in my book, **30 Days to a Clean and Organized House**.)

To clean your closet, start by discarding all trash. This includes permanently stained clothing!

Dust the ceiling, walls, door jamb, shelves and light fixture.

Pick up everything on the floor then clean the baseboards. Vacuum and mop the floor. Return whatever you store on the floor and arrange it neatly.

Clean smudges on the walls, doors, light switches, and door knobs.

» TIP *If musty odors are a problem, fill a sock with chalk sticks – even sidewalk chalk works. Tie a knot in the end of the sock and put it on your closet shelf to absorb moisture. Replace the chalk every time you clean your closet.*

 *Deck, porch, and patio furniture*

Outdoor furniture gets grimy thanks to its constant exposure to the elements. Cleaning it regularly keeps it looking and feeling nice. As with most household items, regular cleaning will help it last longer, too.

Fill a bowl or bucket with 2 quarts warm water, 1 cup white distilled vinegar, and 2 tablespoons liquid dish detergent. Remove any pillows or cushions from your furniture and set them aside.

Sweep or use a brush to dislodge dirt. Then dip a scrub brush dipped into the soapy water and clean the furniture. Rinse well and let air dry.

To clean the cushions, make a fresh batch of the cleaning solution above and pour it into a spray bottle. Sweep or brush the cushions to dislodge dirt. Spray and scrub them, then rinse them with a hose.

Let the cushions sun dry, turning them over every hour or two, and return them to place.

 *Gutters*

Depending on where you live, you might be able to put this task off to merely twice a year. I live in Kansas where spring sends cottonwood fluff and other debris flying, summer storms toss tree branches around, autumn showers us with leaves, and winter brings more flying branches. In short, when the weather isn't trying to kill us it's clogging our gutters, so I clean our gutters every 3 months.

If climbing on a ladder and scooping junk with your hands isn't appealing, there are nifty gadgets you can attach to your leaf blower that will do a decent job of clearing most debris from your gutter. (See my Recommended Product page on HousewifeHowTos.com.)

If you do use one of those attachments, make sure you aren't simply blowing the debris into your downspouts or you'll clog them.

 *Attic*

Whether you use your attic for storage or not, you need to inspect and clean it annually for signs of rodent damage.

Remember: mice can squeeze through an opening as small as a dime! Fill any holes you find with stainless steel – which mice can't stand – then spackle them closed.

Sweep your attic ceiling and walls to get rid of cobwebs and insect nests, then clean the tops of any boxes you've stored in there, and finally sweep the floor.

>> **TIP** *Deter mice, cockroaches, moths, spiders, and silverfish by soaking squares of flannel cloth in peppermint essential oil. Leave these in your attic corners and place a few along the rafters – they hate the smell!*

Fireplace and chimney

Make sure it's been at least 12 hours since you last burned anything in your fireplace so the ashes are completely cool!

Spread a drop cloth or newspapers on the floor.

Sprinkle damp coffee grounds liberally over the ashes to keep them from flying around as you scoop them up. Using a fireplace brush or hand broom, sweep the ashes into a fireproof bucket. Add them to your compost pile or sprinkle them in the garden to add nutrients to your soil. Sweep the screens, too.

To clean smoke and soot stains, first put on rubber or latex cleaning gloves because this is *messy*.

Mix 1 cup hot water, 1 cup hot white distilled vinegar, and 1 tablespoon liquid dish detergent in a spray bottle. In a large bowl or bucket, stir 1 cup baking soda (bicarbonate of soda) into 2 quarts hot water until it dissolves.

Spray the walls of the firebox well with the first solution, then use a scrub brush to scour the soot. Rinse the scrub brush in the bowl of water (there may be a little fizzing) and spray the walls again to rinse. Repeat as needed, dumping out the bowl and refilling it as necessary.

While the firebox dries, spray and scrub the screens and glass, along with the grate that holds the logs. If you have a gas fireplace with faux logs, use a paintbrush or toothbrush to dust them. Washing is not necessary.

Unless you have the tools to do it, and don't mind climbing on your roof, don't try cleaning your chimney yourself!

Chimneys need to be inspected annually for squirrel and bird nests, leaves, creosote buildup and dangerous leaks that can fill your home with carbon monoxide or cause structural fires.

As much a fan of DIY as I am, this is one task I urge you to leave to the professionals. (At $75-150, it's worth it.)

 *Curtains*

Shaking your curtains at the start of your weekly cleaning will do a good job of keeping them mostly free of pet hair, lint, and dust. It's still a good idea to wash them once a year, though, and doing so will help your rooms smell fresh, too.

Follow the manufacturer's label if you can find it. Otherwise, launder unlined garment fabric curtains two panels at a time on a cool/cool gentle cycle using half as much laundry detergent as usual. Dry them on a low-heat cycle then remove and hang them as soon as the cycle ends.

Sheer and lace curtains tend to snag in the washing machine so they're best laundered one panel at a time in the sink or tub using cool water and a tablespoon of liquid detergent. Let them soak for 10 minutes then rinse well. Gently squeeze out as much moisture as possible then hang them while they're still damp so they dry without wrinkles. Place towels beneath them to catch drips.

> **» TIP** *To give sheers a nice crisp feel, add 1 cup Epsom salt to the rinse water. Do not rinse this out. Squeeze and hang as above.*

Clean acrylic bead or shell curtains in place to avoid tangles. Spread a towel beneath to catch drips. Combine 2 cups warm water and a few drops of liquid detergent in a spray bottle, then spray the curtains top to bottom. Wipe with a damp microfiber cloth to dislodge dirt.

Velvet or lined curtains should be dry cleaned. This can cost around $40-60 per panel, which is why I switched to washable curtains.

If that expense exceeds your budget, as it did mine, you can still get your curtains clean by holding them taut with one hand and running your vacuum cleaner with the dust brush attachment from top to bottom.

Spot clean obvious stains with a white damp cloth and cool, soapy water.

Behind heavy furniture

Once a year, as you do your weekly cleaning, you should move heavy furniture and clean behind it. T

This also gives you a chance to treat any dust rings that have formed around the furniture. (It happens to the best of us.)

Be sure to get help with this if you have a bad back!

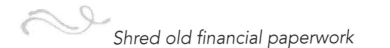 *Shred old financial paperwork*

Laws concerning how long you need to hold onto financial documents vary, so familiarize yourself with your country's rules.

After that, don't hold onto paperwork you no longer need to keep – shred it or burn it, but get it out of your house. I like to do this right after mailing in my taxes for the year – something about ripping and shredding things to bits at that point perks me up.

PHEW!

Was that a bunch of dry reading or what? Still, like I said at the beginning of this section, the idea is to help you understand *why* and *how* things should be cleaned, and to give you an idea of *when* to clean them. Use that section as a reference when planning your own cleaning routines.

Speaking of which, let's talk about different cleaning routine options to give you ideas about creating one that works for you. Ready?

PART TWO:

FINDING YOUR ROUTINE

If you've spent any time Googling for home cleaning routines, you already know that no two people seem to follow the same one. That's because – and I can't emphasize this enough – **the only "correct" cleaning routine is the one that works for YOU to keep YOUR home up to YOUR standards!**

There's no one else to please.

There are no clean house awards, no celebrity judges who'll come to your home and run a white gloved finger over your doorjamb to see how often you're dusting. (Thank goodness for that, too!)

So, as you look over the examples of cleaning routines, don't see them as accusations or even ideals. They're tools – nothing more, nothing less – to help you find a routine that works with your schedule, energy levels, and standards.

Most importantly, it's about finding a routine that helps you achieve these things and *still* have time to enjoy life.

EXAMPLES OF CLEANING ROUTINES

As you browse the following examples of cleaning routines, feel free to pick and choose from them to craft one that works for *you*. When you find a routine that truly fits your schedule you'll be able to stick with it, and that means you'll finally have your home under control.

THE TRADITIONAL ROUTINE

Fans of _The Little House in the Prairie books_ will recognize the traditional routine as the one Ma taught Laura and Mary to follow. Ma had, in turn, learned it from her mother who'd probably learned it from her own mother, and so on.

It went like this:

Mondays – Laundry
Tuesdays – Ironing
Wednesdays – Mending
Thursdays – Churning butter
Fridays – Cleaning
Saturdays – Baking
Sundays - Resting

Now, keep in mind that "laundry" meant washing clothes in a huge vat using lye soap, boiling water, and a washboard then line-drying them. "Ironing" involved a heavy iron that was heated on the wood stove, even in the middle of summer. Mending was a necessity: farm life was hard on clothes and clothes were handmade. As for cleaning on Fridays? When you live in a two-room home and your bathroom is an outhouse it doesn't even take an entire day.

Over the next 50 years homes grew bigger, plumbing moved indoors, and inventions like the electric iron, washing machines and dryers, refrigeration, and vacuum cleaners radically changed housekeeping schedules.

The schedule followed by our grandmothers (or great-grandmothers, depending on your age) looked like this:

Mondays – Laundry
Tuesdays – Ironing
Wednesdays – Shopping and other errands
Thursday – Top floor
Friday – Main floor
Saturdays – Baking

So, how would a Traditional schedule look now with our abundance of modern appliances and the list of daily chores covered earlier? Probably something like this.

Every day:

Kitchen: Wash dishes, clean the kitchen sink, counters, and floor, change kitchen dish cloths and towels, microwave sponges

Bedrooms: Make beds, put dirty clothes in hampers, take water glasses and dishes to kitchen

Bathrooms: Clean toilet messes, wipe vanity and sinks, change hand towels

Living/Family Room or Lounge: Pick up dishes and trash, fold blankets and straighten throw pillows, straighten items on coffee table and side tables, wipe up spills and crumbs.

Mondays – Laundry

Tuesdays – Monthly, 3-month, or annual chore (M/3/A)

Wednesdays – Shopping and errands + entryway

Thursdays – Top floor + M/3/A

Fridays – Main floor + M/3/A
Saturdays and Sundays – Rest

Pros and Cons

Doing all your laundry on Monday means you are doing laundry *all day* on Monday. You can, of course, use one of the weekend days to do a few loads, but be sure to follow-through with putting them away or you won't be able to relax and enjoy your home on the weekend.

If you have small children, you already know they make messes as fast as you can clean them. With this schedule, you're only cleaning the main rooms in your home on Thursdays and Fridays – the other days you'll need to be okay with a little mess.

THE "LITTLE EACH DAY" ROUTINE

The idea behind this routine is to spend less time cleaning on a day-to-day basis, but you wind up doing chores on the weekend.

Every day:

Kitchen: Wash dishes, clean the kitchen sink, wipe counters, spot treat the floor, change kitchen dish cloths and towels, microwave sponges

Bedrooms: Make beds, put dirty clothes in hampers, take water glasses and dishes to kitchen

Bathrooms: Clean toilet messes, wipe vanity and sinks, change hand towels

Living/Family Room or Lounge: Pick up dishes and trash, fold blankets and straighten throw pillows, straighten items on coffee table and side tables, wipe up spills and crumbs.

Mondays – Weekly kitchen cleaning + M/3/A + wash kitchen linens

Tuesdays – Weekly bathroom cleaning + M/3/A + bathroom towels

Wednesdays – Shopping and errands + entryway

Thursdays – Weekly living/family room cleaning + M/3/A

Fridays – Weekly bedroom cleaning + sheets

Saturdays – Wash, fold, and put away clothes

Sundays – Rest

Pros and Cons

This schedule works very well for people with chronic illness since it paces housework throughout the week. For the curious, this is the schedule I follow and that's precisely why: I have psoriatic arthritis which flares horribly when I don't pace myself.

For the same reason, those whose work schedules are unpredictable may find this approach works, too.

The first week or two of following it *will take longer* as you establish a baseline clean using the weekly cleaning checklists. After that, however, you'll discover that weekly vacuuming means your furniture isn't as dusty, cleaning kitchen grime doesn't involve as much scrubbing, and cleaning the shower or tub is a breeze when you don't have to scour grout and mildew.

That said, this schedule requires diligence. Following it for one week then ignoring it for the next week or two means you aren't establishing a baseline. Every time you break the weekly cycle you need to be prepared for the next cleaning to take longer.

THE WEEKENDER ROUTINE

If your job is physically or mentally challenging – and that includes keeping up with kids all day! – you might find the Weekender Routine suits you best.

You're not completely ignoring your home the other five days per week – you've still got daily tasks, after all – but the bulk of your cleaning *and laundry* gets done on the weekend.

Every day:

Kitchen*:* Wash dishes, clean the kitchen sink, wipe counters, spot treat the floor, change kitchen dish cloths and towels, microwave sponges

Bedrooms*:* Make beds, put dirty clothes in hampers, take water glasses and dishes to kitchen

Bathrooms*:* Clean toilet messes, wipe vanity and sinks, change hand towels

Living/Family Room or Lounge*:* Pick up dishes and trash, fold blankets and straighten throw pillows, straighten items on coffee table and side tables, wipe up spills and crumbs.

Monday – Friday: Daily tasks

Saturday – Bathrooms and bedrooms + 2 monthly/3 month/annual (M/3/A) chores + launder bathroom linens and sheets

Sunday – Kitchen and living/family room or lounge and entryway + 2 M/3/A chores + launder kitchen linens and clothing

Pros and Cons

This schedule eats up your weekend, so if you don't find opportunities to relax during the week you'll quickly burn out. Also, skipping a weekend due to illness or exhaustion means you'll have to put up with a mess all week.

If you have small children, you may find it challenging to spend basically all day on Saturday and Sunday cleaning and doing laundry unless you have a partner willing to take over with the kids while you clean.

On the other hand, if your kids are older this schedule combined with the Cleaning Checklists makes it easy to enlist their help!

THE PERFECTIONIST

I'm including this schedule because there are some people who want their home to be spotless *all the time*. I'm not one of them, but I understand the desire.

I'm all about finding your own "good enough" and for some that means perfection, or as close as they can get to it. If that's your goal but you haven't found a schedule to achieve it, this will get you off to a good start.

Do note that the list of daily tasks is *much* longer for the Perfectionist Cleaning Routine. However, because so much is being done daily, the weekly tasks go quickly.

Every day:

Kitchen: Wash dishes, clean the kitchen sink and counters, wipe appliance fronts, clean up spills in the refrigerator, change kitchen dish cloths and towels, microwave sponges, clean the microwave, sweep and mop the floor.

Bedrooms: Make beds, put dirty clothes in hampers, take water glasses and dishes to kitchen, dust horizontal surfaces, vacuum high traffic areas.

Bathrooms: Clean toilet messes, scrub the toilet bowl, wipe vanity and sinks, buff water spots on mirrors, squeegee shower and glass shower doors, clean the tub, change hand towels, sweep and mop the floor.

Living/Family Room or Lounge: Pick up dishes and trash, fold blankets and straighten throw pillows, straighten items on coffee table and side tables, wipe up spills and crumbs, dust horizontal surfaces, vacuum high traffic areas.

Entryway: Pick up shoes and return extras to where they belong, hang coats, clean smudges on storm door, polish doorknob, sweep and mop.

Laundry: Wash at least one load of clothing, fold or iron, and put away.

Whole house: Empty all wastebaskets.

Monday: Weekly kitchen cleaning + 1 monthly/3 month/annual chore (M/3/A) + wash kitchen linens

Tuesdays – Weekly bathroom cleaning + 1 M/3/A chore + wash bathroom towels and rugs

Wednesdays – Shopping and errands + weekly entryway cleaning

Thursdays – Weekly living/family room or lounge cleaning + M/3/A

Fridays – Weekly bedroom cleaning + M/3/A + wash sheets

Saturdays – Wash, fold, and put away clothes + M/3/A

Sundays - Rest

Pros and Cons

Depending on the size of your home and how many people and pets live in it, this schedule can feel like a full-time job – and probably will be.

If you follow this schedule for a while and find yourself wanting to ease up a bit, do so! The Little Each Day routine will still keep your home looking nice, and you can always add in a few random additional tasks if you see a mess that bothers you.

CREATING YOUR PERSONALIZED ROUTINE

Now that you've seen examples of possible cleaning routines, it's time to find one that suits your schedule, your energy levels, and your standards. The worksheets below will help.

>>**TIP** *If you're reading this on a Kindle Fire 3rd generation or later, you can take a screenshot of the worksheets by pressing the Volume Down and Power Buttons at the same time. Then go to your Photo App and look under "Screenshots." From there, you can print them!*

If you're reading this on an iPhone, press Volume and Power simultaneously to take screenshots. You can print them from the photo app.

If you're reading the paperback, I've left room for your answers, so grab a pen!

 *Discover What Matters To YOU*

Finding a cleaning routine for *your* schedule involves understanding your own standards. If you've tried following someone else's routine only to find yourself frustrated, it's because *their* routine did not reflect *your* priorities.

So, let's take a few moments to discover what those priorities are.

It is perfectly fine to have rooms in your home you could not possibly care less about. That doesn't mean you don't want them clean now and then – it simply means that's not a room worth focusing a lot of your time and effort on.

In my home, for example, I couldn't care less what my teenage son's room looks like for the most part. If there are no vile odors coming out of it, and I'm not missing too many dishes, I ignore it entirely.

Every now and then, though, I do expect him to clean it. (That's when I hand him the Bedroom Weekly Cleaning Checklist to follow, regardless how long it's been since his room was last cleaned.)

Maybe you have different rooms you don't care much about. Identifying them now will help you give them lower priority when developing your own cleaning routine.

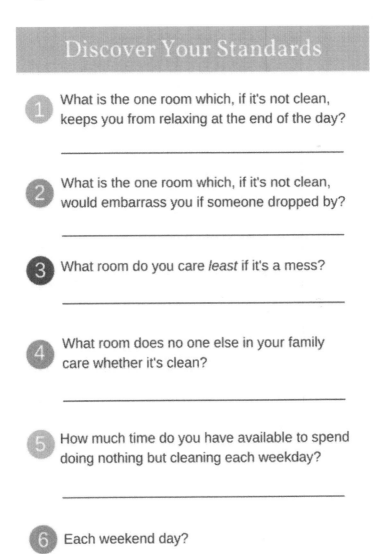

Discover Your Standards

1 What is the one room which, if it's not clean, keeps you from relaxing at the end of the day?

_____

2 What is the one room which, if it's not clean, would embarrass you if someone dropped by?

_____

3 What room do you care *least* if it's a mess?

_____

4 What room does no one else in your family care whether it's clean?

_____

5 How much time do you have available to spend doing nothing but cleaning each weekday?

_____

6 Each weekend day?

_____

The Priority Matrix

Room you need clean for YOU	Room you want clean for visitors
Room YOU don't care about	Room no one else cares about

Prioritize Your Cleaning

Top rooms in matrix = 1 and 2
All other rooms get 3 (highest) to 8 (lowest)

Kitchen _____
Your bathroom _____
Kids' bathroom _____
Guest bathroom _____
Your bedroom _____
Kids' bedrooms _____
Living Room _____
Entryway _____

92

This is your priority matrix. The top row represents the rooms where you need to focus most of your time and energy.

Aim to schedule the weekly cleaning of these rooms early in the week and then give them a little extra attention before the weekend. This way you'll have a clean, comfortable spot to relax and can feel confident that anyone who comes over will enjoy your home, too.

The bottom two rows are your low-impact rooms. You don't care as much about them, and neither does anyone else. *It's good to recognize this!* Schedule these rooms later in the week, so if something unexpected comes up that throws your schedule out of whack it won't bother you as much.

By assigning a value to each room (1 through 8 in the above worksheet) you're making decisions about the order in which you want to clean the rooms of your home. This helps focus your efforts on the rooms that matter most to you early in the week, when you have energy and are motivated.

The rooms lower in the list still need cleaning, of course, but they won't have as great of an impact on your comfort and home confidence level. Putting them later in the week means you'll still get to them but, if you can't put your all into them and their associated M/3/A chores, it won't bother you as much.

Before you write down your own personal cleaning schedule, there are a couple more questions you should ask yourself.

Structuring your routine to fit YOUR schedule

Structuring Your Routine

Write your priority list in numerical order

1. _____
2. _____
3. _____
4. _____
5. _____
6. _____
7. _____
8. _____

Additional Considerations

What day do you want to grocery shop?

_____

What day do you want to wash clothing?

_____

What day(s) do you want to skip cleaning?

_____

So now, keeping these answers in mind, let's create your own personalized cleaning schedule!

Remember: Higher importance rooms and tasks should be scheduled early in the week (M-W) while lower importance rooms and tasks belong later in the week (Th-S).

Remember to note which days you'll do M/3/A tasks, too.

YOUR PERSONALIZED WEEKLY ROUTINE

Weekly Cleaning Routine

Mon.

Tues.

Wed.

Thurs.

Fri.

Sat.

Su

Hang your personalized Weekly Cleaning Schedule on your refrigerator or somewhere else you're sure to see it.

You've made a commitment to yourself – now it's time to put it into practice with the Cleaning Checklists!

PART THREE:

CHECKLISTS AND RECIPES

Now that you've created your personalized weekly cleaning schedule, it's time to finally get started. The checklists below will guide you through all the daily, weekly, monthly, quarterly, and annual tasks – just find the one you need and off you go!

You're certainly free to use whatever commercial products work best for you. I've included several homemade cleaning solution recipes in this section for those who prefer such things.

The Recommended Products page on HousewifeHowTos.com lists all the cleaning tools I use when cleaning my own home, along with the supplies I prefer for making homemade cleaning mixes. (Note to readers outside the US: I'm unable to provide direct links for your use, but you can use my recommendations to search for equivalent products.)

CLEANING CHECKLISTS

» **TIP** *If you're reading this on a Kindle Fire 3ʳᵈ generation or later, you can take a screenshot of the worksheets by pressing the Volume Down and Power Buttons at the same time. Then go to your Photo App and look under "Screenshots." From there, you can print them!*

If you're reading this on an iPhone, press Volume and Power simultaneously to take screenshots. You can print them from the photo app.

Daily Routine

Whether you do your daily tasks in the morning or before bed, the important thing is to do them *every* day. This practice will keep your home looking tidy between weekly cleanings and, in fact, will make those weekly cleanings go faster!

Daily Cleaning

Kitchen

Wash dishes | Sweep floor
Clean sink | Spot clean floor
Wipe Counters | Change towels
Microwave sponge | Change dish cloth

Optional: Wipe small appliance and appliance fronts

Bedroom

Make bed
Pick up dirty clothes
Take dishes to sink

Optional: Vacuum high-traffic areas

Living Room

Take dishes to sink | Fold blankets
Pick up trash | Straighten pillows
Wipe messes | Neaten DVDs, etc.

Optional: Vacuum high-traffic areas

Bathroom

Clean toilet messes
Clean sinks & faucets
Change hand towels

Optional: Wipe vanity, buff mirror, spray shower

Kitchen Weekly Cleaning

Prep

Put trash in bin
Gather clutter
Wash dishes

Scrub sink
Run ice in disposal
Microwave wet sponge

Spray & Wipe

Cupboard fronts
Drawer fronts
Countertops
Backsplash
Small appliances

Appliance fronts
Top of refrigerator
Light switches
Phone
Outside of garbage can

Clean

Microwave
Toss expired food
Wipe spills in fridge & freezer
Change liner in refrigerator drawers
Sweep and mop floor

Finish

Empty trash
Change towels
Change dish cloth
Return clutter to where it belongs

Bathroom Weekly Cleaning

Prep

Put trash in bin	Clear vanity
Put away toiletries	Dust light fixture
Gather clutter	Dry wipe surfaces
Clear tub surround	Use toilet bowl cleaner

Spray

Scrub toilet bowl	Tub surround
Flush toilet	Tub
Vanity	Shower
Sinks	Tank and outside of toilet
Faucets	Seat and lid of toilet

Wipe

All sprayed surfaces
Polish shower doors
Polish chrome fixtures
Clean mirror

Finish

Sweep and mop floor
Change towels
Empty trash
Check supplies
Return clutter to where it belongs

Bedroom Weekly Cleaning

Prep

Put trash in bin
Gather clutter
Dishes to kitchen
Remove bedspread
Shake curtains well

Dust

Blinds, both sides
Window casings
Window sills
Wall art
Mirror
Furniture
Lamp shades
Lamp bulbs
Lamps

Wipe

Smudges on walls
Door knobs
Door jambs
Light switches
TV remote

Finish

Change sheets
Make bed
Vacuum floor
Empty trash
Return clutter to where it belongs

Living Room Weekly Cleaning

Prep

Put trash in bin
Gather clutter
Dishes to kitchen
Fold blankets

Toss old magazines
Put away DVDs, etc.
Shake curtains

Dust

Blinds, both sides
Window casings
Window sills
Wall art
TV screen

Furniture
Lamp shades
Lamp bulbs
Lamps

Wipe

Smudges on walls
Door knobs
Door jambs
Light switches
TV remote

Finish

Vacuum furniture
Vacuum floor
Empty trash
Return clutter to where it belongs

Entryway Weekly Cleaning

Prep
Put trash in bin
Gather clutter
Hang coats
Straighten shoes

Wipe

Smudges on walls	Storm door
Door knobs	Door knocker
Door jambs	Door
Light switches	Furniture

Sweep
Screens
Cobwebs in corners
Mats
Floor

Finish
Mop floor
Return clutter to where it belongs

Dishwasher Cleaning - Monthly

Prep
Remove racks
Inspect bottom of unit for debris
Make sure spray arms spin freely
Inspect sprayers for debris

Wash
Remove and wash food catcher
Spread and clean door gasket
Drain machine
Add 2 cups vinegar to bottom of unit
Run short hot cycle

Finish
Return food catcher
Return racks
Wipe exterior

Optional: Fill rinse agent dispenser with vinegar

Oven Cleaning - Monthly

Prep
Remove racks
Scrape up burned-on food
Run self-cleaning cycle if any

Clean
Make paste of baking soda & water
Scour food spills
Wipe with damp paper towel
Use hot, soapy water to clean interior
Wipe with clean, damp paper towels

Tough Spots
Combine equal parts of water & vinegar
Soap paper towel in this mixture
Place towel on spots to soak
Wipe clean

Finish
Wash racks in sink
Scour spots with baking soda & water
Rinse and dry racks
Return racks to place

Fridge/Freezer Cleaning - Monthly

Prep
Unplug the unit
Remove everything from the front
Transfer contents to coolers
Pull the unit out from the wall
Dump ice container into sink

Wash
Ice container
Shelves
Drawers
Gasket
Exterior of unit

Sweep
Sweep and mop behind unit
Vacuum coils
Return unit to place and plug in
Sweep floor
Mop floor

Finish
Toss expired food
Put new liner in drawers
Reinstall ice container
Return food to unit
Return items to front of unit

Laundry Room Cleaning - Monthly

Prep
Put trash in bin
Gather clutter
Dust all surfaces to remove lint

Spray & Wipe

Smudges on walls	Blinds - both sides
Door knobs	Outside of machines
Door jambs	Washer drum & gasket
Light switches	Dryer drum
Window sills	Clean lint screen

Sweep
Pull machines out from wall
Sweep and mop behind them
Unhook dryer vent hose and clean
Return machines to place
Sweep and mop floor

Finish
Check supplies
Reinstall clean lint screen
Empty trash
Return clutter to where it belongs

Garage Cleaning - Monthly

Prep
Pull cars out of garage
Pick up trash
Gather items that belong elsewhere

Dust & Wipe
Dust light fixtures
Dust stored items
Wipe light switches
Wipe door smudges
Wipe door jamb

Treat Spots
Sprinkle oil spots with clay kitty litter
Wait for litter to soak up surface oil
Sweep up litter
Wash spot with hot, soapy water
Let dry

Finish
Shake entry mats
Sweep mats
Sweep walls
Sweep floor
Pull cars back in

Car Monthly Cleaning

Car Cleaning - Monthly

Prep
Throw away trash
Gather clutter (including in trunk) - set aside
Remove floor mats - set aside

Vacuum
Ceiling
Seats - on, under, between
Console & cupholders
Dashboard
Floor and mats

Wipe

Dashboard	*Combine:*
Console	1 cup water
Door panels	1 cup vinegar
Seatbelt buckles	1 tsp. liquid dish soap
Steering wheel	Spray and scrub stains

Finish
Clean windows
Polish chrome accents
Return mats to place
Shine dashboard & leather (optional)

Homemade Armor All: Equal parts water, vinegar & baby oil

Deck & Patio Furniture - Quarterly

Prep

Remove pillows and cushions
Combine in bowl:
2 quarts warm water
1 cup white distilled vinegar
2 tablespoons liquid dish detergent

Clean

Brush or sweep furniture to dislodge dirt
Use scrub brush dipped in mixture to wash
Rinse with clear water
Let fully dry

Pillows

Sweep or vacuum to dislodge dust
Make half batch of cleaning solution
Pour into spray bottle
Spray pillows with solution
Scrub with brush
Rinse with fresh water

Finish

Turn pillows hourly while they dry
Return pillows to place

Misc. Monthly Cleaning

Ceiling Fans

Turn fan off
Slip pillowcase over each blade to dust *or*
Use extension dusting kit's fan brush

Set fans counter-clockwise in summer, clockwise in winter

Blinds

Put towel on floor
Wrap ends of kitchen tongs with cloths
Secure cloths with rubber bands
Dip tong ends in cleaner
Run tongs horizontally along each slat

Cleaner: 1 cup water, 1 cup rubbing alcohol, 1 tsp. dish soap

Drains

Prime tap by running water until hot
Turn off water
Pour one-half cup baking soda into drain
Slowly pour 2 cups hot vinegar into drain
When fizzing stops, run hot water

Baseboards

Use extension cleaning kit's duster or
Dust brush on vacuum cleaner
Wash spots with all-purpose cleaner

Bedroom Closet - Quarterly

Purge

Clothes that don't fit
Clothes that don't flatter
Clothes that aren't comfortable
Clothes that don't make you feel good
Clothes with permanent stains

Prep

Throw away trash
Gather items that belong elsewhere
Collect empty hangers, take to laundry room

Clean

Dust shelves
Dust light fixture
Dust door
Dust door jamb
Wipe smudges

Finish

Pick everything up from floor
Sweep or vacuum floor
Mop
Return items to floor

Treat musty odors by storing a chalk-filled sock on the shelf.

Bedding - Quarterly

Pillows
Wash 2 at a time using hot cycle
Use 1/2 normal amount of detergent
Add 1/2 cup each oxy-bleach & baking soda
Add 1 cup vinegar to rinse cycle
Rinse again with just water
Dry 2 at a time with tennis balls to fluff

Blankets
Follow label instructions, if any
Wash cotton & synthetics in warm/warm
Wash quilts on delicate cycle in cold/cold
Tumble dry low

Mattress
Vacuum
Sprinkle with baking soda & work it in
Vacuum again
Flip side to side in spring, fall
Flip end to end in summer, winter

Mattress Stains
Blood: Paste of 3% hydrogen peroxide & 1 tbsp. each liquid dish soap and salt. Let dry. Vacuum up.

Urine: Spray with 3 tbsp. baking soda, 8 oz. hydrogen peroxide & 2 drops liquid dish soap. Wipe.

Always use a white cloth to avoid transferring dye.

Air Ducts - Quarterly

Prep
Remove floor registers
Wash registers in hot, soapy water. Rinse.
Let registers air dry while you work.

Clean
Insert vacuum hose or tool into duct
Work hose or tool around to clean all sides
Wipe as far as you can reach into ducts

Finish
Let ducts fully dry
Return dry registers to place
Run whole-house fan to filter loosened dust
Change air filter

Shampoo Carpet - Quarterly

Prep
Move any small furniture out of room
Use crevice tool at base of walls
Use crevice tool at base of heavy furniture
Vacuum floor thoroughly

Pretreat
Combine 1 cup warm water & 1 cup vinegar
Add 1/2 teaspoon liquid dish detergent
Use white cloth to dab this onto stains
Wait 5 minutes
Blot with clean, dry white cloth

Shampoo
Use HOT water when mixing shampoo
Work s-l-o-w-l-y
Do not oversaturate
Work in overlapping sections across room
Let carpet fully dry before repeating sections!

Finish
Let carpet fully dry
Vacuum again to fluff carpet fibers
Return small furniture to place

Misc. Quarterly Cleaning

Gutters
Do not work alone if you're using a ladder
Wear gloves to protect your hands
Scoop leaves out of gutters with hands
Or use attachment on leaf blower
Avoid clogging downspouts with debris

Windows
Work on an overcast day
Place towel beneath windows indoors
Spray with glass cleaner then use squeegee
Work in opposite directions inside & out
Use spray and microfiber cloth on streaks

Coffee Makers
Unplug machine
Clean exterior using microfiber cloth
Use soapy water (sparingly) on hot plate
Fill tank with equal parts water and vinegar
Run full cycle of vinegar water and discard
Run several cycles of plain water

Medicine Cabinet
Discard products you don't use
Discard products you don't like
Remove everything, wipe shelves
Check remaining product expiration dates
Add needed refills to shopping list
Return items to cabinet

Curtain Cleaning - Annual

Prep
Remove curtains
If using a ladder, do not work alone
Check manufacturer's label for instructions
Spot test for colorfastness before washing!

Unlined cloth
Wash 2 panels at a time
Use the gentle cycle and cold water
Dry on low heat
Remove from dryer promptly and rehang

Sheers & Lace
Wash by hand in sink
Use cool water and 1 tbsp. liquid detergent
Let soak 10 minutes then drain
Add more cold water and 1 cup Epsom salt
Soak 10 minutes
Gently squeeze out excess water
Put towel on floor and rehang sheers to dry

Bead
Leave hanging
Place towel on floor beneath curtain
Fill spray bottle with warm water
Add 2-3 drops liquid dish soap
Spray bead curtain top to bottom
Wipe with clean, damp cloth

Fireplace Cleaning - Annual

Prep
Wait at least 12 hours after last fire
Place drop cloth or towel on floor
Sprinkle damp coffee grounds over ashes
Sweep ashes into fireproof bucket or can
For gas fireplace, remove logs and rocks
Remove log holder

Mix
In spray bottle:
1 cup hot water
1 cup white vinegar
1 tbsp. dish soap

In bowl:
1 cup baking soda
2 quarts hot water

Wear rubber or latex gloves while cleaning.

Spray & Scrub
Spray walls of firebox until saturated
Scrub walls with brush, rinse brush in bowl
Repeat until walls are clean
Spray and scrub floor of firebox
Spray and scrub screens, glass doors
Spray and scrub log holder

Finish
Let firebox air dry
Use brush to dislodge dust on gas logs
Return log holder (and gas logs, if any)
Schedule professional chimney cleaning

Misc. Annual Cleaning

Attic
Inspect for signs of rodent damage
Stuff stainless steel into rodent holes
Sweep ceiling and walls to remove cobwebs
Dust stored objects
Sweep the floor
Scatter flannel squares soaked in peppermint oil to deter pests

Behind Furniture
Get help to move heavy furniture
Dust wall behind item
Dust baseboard
Dust back of item
Vacuum floor
Return item to place

Old Papers
Look up law on document retention
Gather papers you don't need to keep
Shred papers
Add shreds to compost, burn/discard them
File remaining paperwork

Recipes

NOTE

Most of the cleaning recipes call for two or more of the following ingredients:

White vinegar
Rubbing alcohol (surgical spirits)
Liquid dish soap (Dawn or Fairy)
Hydrogen peroxide 3%
Baking soda (bicarbonate of soda)
Essential oils

The proportions of ingredients change based on the recipe's function. In some cases, weaker solutions are needed to avoid damaging surfaces in your home.

If you don't want to have several bottles of different cleaners, stick with the all-purpose cleaner, disinfectant spray, furniture polish, and glass cleaner.

>> TIP *If you're reading this on a Kindle Fire 3rd generation or later, you can take a screenshot of the worksheets by pressing the Volume Down and Power Buttons at the same time. Then go to your Photo App and look under "Screenshots." From there, you can print them!*

If you're reading this on an iPhone, press Volume and Power simultaneously to take screenshots. You can print them from the photo app.

Air Freshener Spray

Air Freshener Spray

Home fragrance without the harsh ingredients.

Ingredients

2 oz. vodka
2 oz. water
20-30 drops essential oil

Directions

1. *Combine ingredients in spray bottle*
2. *Swirl before use*
3. *Avoid use on silk, satin, and velvet*
4. *Store away from light*

Combinations to try:
15 drops lavender, 10 drops lemon
8 drops each cinnamon, sweet orange, bergamot
15 drops sweet orange, 10 sage
15 drops rose, 10 sandalwood

125

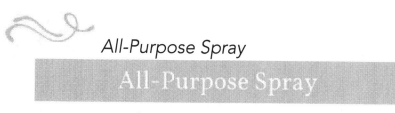

All-Purpose Spray

All-Purpose Spray

Cleans surfaces that don't require disinfection.

Ingredients

16 oz. water
4 oz. white vinegar
Juice of one lemon (must be fresh), strained
5-10 drops lemon essential oil (optional)

Directions

1. Combine ingredients in spray bottle
2. Use on counters, faucets, appliances
3. Spray on surfaces and wipe immediately
4. Store spray away from light
5. DO NOT USE ON NATURAL STONE

Bed Linen Spray

Bed Linen Spray

Every night can smell like Clean Sheet Night!

Ingredients

1 oz. witch hazel
3 oz. water
5-10 drops essential oil
(lavender or sandalwood are nice)

Directions

1. Combine ingredients in spray bottle
2. Swirl before use
3. Spray linens lightly -- don't get your bed wet!
4. Avoid use on silk, satin, and velvet
5. Store away from light

Carpet Shampoo

Carpet Shampoo

Spot test before use!

Ingredients

2 quarts very hot water

2 quarts distilled white vinegar

2 oz. oxygenated bleach* (Oxiclean)

1 teaspoon liquid dish soap (Dawn or Fairy)

Directions

1. Combine ingredients in machine's tank
2. Follow instructions on machine's use
3. No need to rinse

* Oxygenated bleach does not lighten fabrics.

Daily Shower Spray

Daily Shower Spray

Use after showers to prevent mold, mildew, and soap scum

Ingredients

4 oz. hydrogen peroxide
4 oz. rubbing alcohol (surgical spirits in UK)
2-3 drops liquid dish soap (Dawn or Fairy)
1 cup water

Directions

1. Combine ingredients in spray bottle
2. Spray shower walls, floor, and doors
3. No need to wipe or squeegee
4. Store spray away from light and heat

Daily Sink Spray

Daily Sink Spray

Cleans, disinfects, and deodorizes

Ingredients

4 oz. rubbing alcohol (surgical spirits)
4 oz. water
1/2 tsp. Castile soap
10 drops lemon essential oil
Spray bottle

Directions

1. Combine ingredients in spray bottle
2. Spray on walls and floor of sink
3. Wait 1 minute
4. Wipe with dry cloth. No need to rinse.
5. Keep spray away from light and heat

Disinfectant Spray

Disinfectant Spray

Disinfect and clean at the same time.

Ingredients

8 oz. water
8 oz. white vinegar
2 to 3 drops liquid dish soap
15 drops tea tree oil (melaleuca)
Spray bottle

Directions

1. Combine ingredients in spray bottle
2. Spray to saturate surfaces
3. Wait 5 minutes before wiping
4. Store unused solution away from light
5. Do NOT use on natural stone surfaces!

Floor Cleaner

Hard Floor Cleaner

Works on ALL hard floor surfaces!

Ingredients

8 oz. warm water
8 oz. rubbing alcohol (surgical spirits in UK)
4 oz. distilled white vinegar
3 drops liquid dish soap (Dawn or Fairy)
5-10 drops essential oils (optional)

Directions

1. Combine first ingredients in spray bottle
2. Spray floor, use microfiber mop to wipe
3. No need to rinse
4. Double recipe in bucket for large floors
5. Store away from heat and light

Furniture Polish

Furniture Polish

Use after dusting to leave a beautiful shine

Ingredients

8 oz. olive oil
2 oz. white vinegar
3 to 4 drops lemon essential oil (optional)
Spray bottle
Lint-free cloths (flannel diapers work well)

Directions

1. Combine first 3 ingredients in spray bottle
2. Spray cloth then wipe onto furniture to polish
3. Buff with clean lint-free cloth to shine
4. Store remaining polish away from light
   (up to 1 month)

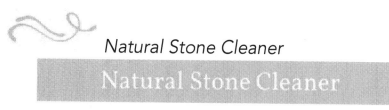

Natural Stone Cleaner

Natural Stone Cleaner

Safe for granite, marble, and other natural stone surfaces

Ingredients

4 oz. rubbing alcohol (surgical spirits in the UK)
12 oz. water
3 drops liquid dish soap (Dawn or Fairy)
10 drops lemon essential oil (optional)

Directions

1. Combine ingredients in spray bottle
2. Spray on surfaces and wipe immediately
3. Store spray away from light and heat

Upholstery Cleaner

Upholstery Cleaner

Use after vacuuming to remove food and ink stains

Ingredients

1 oz. distilled white vinegar
4 oz. rubbing alcohol (surgical spirits in UK)
Spray bottle
Clean white cloths

Directions

1. Combine first 2 ingredients in spray bottle
2. Spray onto stain
3. Use cloth to dab -- not rub -- to lift stain
4. Rotate cloth so you are always working with a clean spot.
5. Once stain is gone, dampen a clean cloth with water and wipe area to neutralize.

Window and Glass Cleaner

Window & Glass Cleaner

Wash windows on an overcast day

Ingredients

8 oz. rubbing alcohol (surgical spirits in UK)
8 oz. white vinegar
3 drops dishwashing liquid (Dawn or Fairy)
Empty spray bottle
Squeegee
Microfiber cloth

Directions

1. Combine first 3 ingredients in spray bottle
2. Spray onto window, use squeegee to wipe
3. For other glass, spray onto microfiber cloth
4. Discard unused cleaner safely

Happy Cleaning!

About the Author

Katie Berry is an author, blogger, mom and homebody who is on a mission to help people learn to turn their homes into havens. She blogs regularly at HousewifeHowTos.com where, in addition to cleaning advice, she also shares delicious family-friendly recipes and money-saving tips.

When she's not reading, Katie can most often be found curled up on the sofa with a book, her dog, and two cats. (She deals with a *lot* of pet hair.)

Subscribe to Katie's free weekly newsletter for cleaning reminders, family menus, and all her latest how-tos. Visit: HousewifeHowTos.com/subscribe

Katie loves social media. Follow her at:
Facebook.com/housewifehowtos
Twitter.com/housewifehowtos
Pinterest.com/housewifehowtos
Instagram.com/housewifehowtos

Other books by Katie Berry (paperback and Kindle)

30 Days to a Clean and Organized House
1,001+ Housewife How-Tos
Autumn: A Season of Easy Cooking

Find out more about Katie's books at:
HousewifeHowTos.com/books

63781920R00078

Made in the USA
Lexington, KY
17 May 2017